Unexplained

Jane
Penrose

Ginn

It's a Mystery!

Somewhere out there, beyond the things we understand, is the weird world of unexplained mysteries. Mysterious events take many different forms – huge patterns appearing in fields, strange lights in the sky, spooky spoon-bending – but they are all equally baffling! Some scientists have ideas about why mysteries *might* happen, but nobody knows for sure. Other people like to blame aliens for these mysteries, but the existence of creatures from outer space is one of the BIGGEST unexplained mysteries of all! Now it's time for you to make your own mind up …

As you fill your mind with mystery, write down and keep your answers to each QUIZ question. (Remember, the answers are in the book!) Now, let's travel into the realm of the UNEXPLAINED!

Are aliens responsible for some unexplained mysteries, or is it unfair to give them the blame?
Did YOU do that?
bwoopp zwip qixik?

The Un-X-plained Files

Are we Alone?

Is there anyone out there?

Messages in the Fields

Take a look at these crazy crop circles ...

Bermuda Triangle BEWARE!

Triangle of Mystery

One minute they were there — the next they were gone!

A Fairy Big Lie!

It's All in the Mind

SWISH!

Jumping Jack Attack!

A Stony Silence

Are we Alone?

Is there life on other planets? And if aliens do exist, would they visit Earth? This unexplained mystery has kept scientists scratching their heads for centuries. Some people think aliens have already visited us, and some even claim to have seen them on their visits! One of the most famous sightings of an alien spaceship, or Unidentified Flying Object (UFO), happened when UFOs and alien creatures seemed to pay a visit to a forest in Suffolk ...

UN-X-PLAINED FILE

Classification: UFO sighting

Location: Rendlesham Forest, Suffolk, UK

Date: 27th–29th December 1980

Witnesses: Workers at the American Air Force and many other locals.

Mystery ranking: Out of this world!

This is an artist's reconstruction of what the Rendlesham Forest UFO might have looked like.

At about 3 a.m. on 27th December 1980, three Air Force patrol guards reported seeing a strange glowing object near their airbase, next to Rendlesham Forest. It was like nothing they had seen before. When the patrol guards scoured the area for clues the next day, they found dents in the ground where the object had been.

Was this a UFO?

Since the Rendlesham Forest sighting, there have been thousands more UFO sightings all over the world. Spaceship-spotters have described the UFOs as being cigar-shaped, looking like carrots, or even being the shape of a bowler hat! But so far, no one has been able to explain the mystery of UFO sightings for sure.

FoRGoTTeN FaCT

People who saw the Rendlesham Forest UFO said that they had 'lost' periods of time and suffered from memory loss, but they didn't forget seeing strange alien creatures in the woods!

Patrol guards found ★★★★★ in the grou

Are you convinced that aliens visit Earth in flying saucers? Well, before you make your mind up, here are some anti-alien theories ...

◎ UFOs are old pieces of rock, called meteorites, which fall to Earth from outer space.

◎ UFOs are strange military aircraft on top-secret missions.

◎ The flashing lights of flying saucers are actually freak weather conditions.

◎ People who claim to have seen UFOs are just great big liars who make it up for attention!

where the mysterious object had been.

Messages in the Fields

Unlike UFO sightings, some mysteries began centuries ago. In 1678, a greedy farmer refused to pay the right wage for crop harvesting, saying he would rather have the devil do the work. The next morning, the farmer woke to find his corn crop had been flattened into **huge** circles and patterns, which no human could have done. The farmer thought the devil had done the work, and was too frightened to collect his corn! **Was this the first crop circle?**

UN-X-PLAINED FILE

Classification: Crop circle

Location: Hertfordshire, UK

Date: Sometime in 1678

Witnesses: One seriously freaked-out farmer

Mystery ranking: Devilishly mysterious!

So what's the big story with crop circles? Some people think that they are messages left for us by aliens. The patterns are extremely neat and very clever, with no evidence of anyone having been in the field. So alien-believers think they are made from above, by UFOs. In the 1980s, more and more crop circles started being found all over the UK, and crop-circle craziness gripped the nation …

One of the most famous crop circles appeared on 14th August 2001, in Wiltshire, and soon got people talking. Witnesses described it as "jaw-dropping and mind-warping", and everyone was flummoxed as to how it was made. The design contained over 400 circles, and appeared overnight, which meant each circle must have taken only 30 seconds to make! Surely impossible for a human? Various pranksters have claimed responsibility, but how the circle was made remains a mystery.

Doug Bower and **** Chorley admitte

So, aliens trying to 'phone home', or clever pranks by corn-benders? Before you decide, take a look at these reasons why there might be nothing out-of-this-world about crop circles.

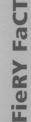

@ **Weird weather** – Mini whirlwinds have been blamed for flattening corn into strange patterns.

@ **Human hoaxers** – Pranksters Doug Bower and Dave Chorley claim that crop circles were a joke invented by them in the 1980s. Another team called the 'Circlemakers' have also admitted making clever crop circles.

FieRY FaCT

Many people have reported seeing fire in the sky on nights when crop circles have appeared, giving fuel to the argument that aliens are to blame. The damage to crops certainly makes farmers red hot with rage!

at they had made crop circles as a joke.

Triangle of Mystery

The legend of Flight 19 is better known as the mystery of the **Bermuda Triangle**. Five Amer bomber planes were on a training mission from Florida in 1945. Everything seemed normal, until flight commander sent a message to base saying that none of the planes' compasses were working properly. Things got weirder at 7:04 p.m. when a communication with Flight 19 was lost. A rescue plane was sent to find them, but that disappeare well! Six planes and 27 men had vanished withou trace! Unusual? Well, maybe not …

UN-X-PLAINED FILE

Classification: Strange disappearance

Location: Bermuda Triangle, Atlantic Ocea

Date: 5th December 1945

Witnesses: They all vanished!

Mystery ranking: Just 'plane' weird!

This is how Flight 19 would have looked, as it flew to its vanishing doom.

Flight 19 was not the first strange disappearance in the area of sea known as the Bermuda Triangle. Way back as far as 1492, the explorer Christopher Columbus said he saw fire in the sky when sailing there, and old maps called the area 'The Devil Islands'. Sounds friendly! Since then, the Bermuda Triangle has been the site of thousands of strange vanishings – ships as well as planes. The **BIG** mystery is where do the missing ships and planes go?

Ships that vamoosh? Planes that go 'poof'? There are plenty of other theories as to why things in the Bermuda Triangle don't seem to hang about for long ...

- ◎ Weather watchers think sudden storms are responsible for the disappearances. The ships and planes quite literally sink without a trace.

- ◎ Twister fans think that huge tornados suck ships and planes up into the sky, before dumping them far away.

- ◎ Sensible spoilsports point out that the Bermuda Triangle doesn't have any more accidents than any other patch of sea. It's just a good story that got carried away ...

A Fairy Big Lie!

In 1918, two mischievous girls caused one of the biggest hoax mysteries in history. Frances Griffiths and Elsie Wright said they had taken photographs of fairies in their garden! The photos were phoney, but many people believed them!

It's All in the Mind

You may think your brain works really hard at school, but we actually only use a small amount of our brainpower. Some people think that the part of the brain we don't use is the part that lets us do amazing things – like reading other people's minds! The scientific name for this mind power is Extra Sensory Perception (ESP). This is when people know something has happened without being told. Lots of people claim to use ESP, but identical twins seem to be better at it than most ...

UN-X-PLAINED FILE

Classification: Extra Sensory Perception

Date: 1979

Witnesses: Identical twins Bridget Harrison of Leicester and Dorothy Lowe of Burnley

Mystery ranking: Mind-boggling!

Don't think at me in that tone of voice!

Identical twins can often tell what each other is thinking, without having to talk.

Bridget Harrison and Dorothy Lowe were identical twins who had been separated at birth. The sisters were reunited when they were 34, and found out about their similar lives. See how closely their brains had been working, even though they were far apart …

Both wore seven rings and two bracelets on one wrist and a watch and bracelet on the other

Both wrote in the same kind of diary, leaving the same days blank

And doubly spooky, one twin had a son called Richard Andrew, and the other had a son called Andrew Richard!

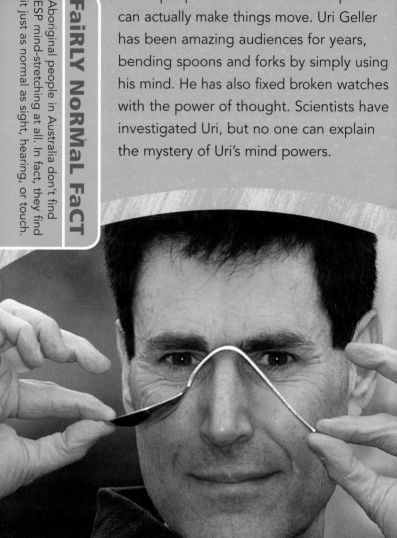

Some people think ESP and mind power can actually make things move. Uri Geller has been amazing audiences for years, bending spoons and forks by simply using his mind. He has also fixed broken watches with the power of thought. Scientists have investigated Uri, but no one can explain the mystery of Uri's mind powers.

FaiRLY NoRMaL FaCT

Aboriginal people in Australia don't find ESP mind-stretching at all. In fact, they find it just as normal as sight, hearing, or touch.

Is your brain in a whirl about ESP, or do believers need their heads testing? Before you make your mind up, take a look at some other theories ...

◎ Identical twins look exactly the same, so it's no surprise that they think the same, too. It's obvious they'd make the same choices and decisions.

◎ Mind reading is easy to fake if you just tell people what you know they'd like to hear.

◎ Making things move with mind power is really just a magic trick, using props.

Jumping Jack Attack!

Imagine someone with the jumping skills of Spiderman, but the mind of an evil stalker. In 1837, a London man was walking home late one night when he saw a man with large glowing eyes jump over railings three metres high! The creature appeared more and more, and soon he was not only scaring people out of their wits, but attacking them too! He would escape by leaping over high walls and onto rooftops, so the terrified Londoners nicknamed him 'Spring-Heeled Jack'.

UN-X-PLAINED FILE

Classification: Mystery high-jumping creature

Location: London, England

Date: 1837 onwards

Witnesses: Many panicked passers-by

Mystery ranking: Sure to make you jump!

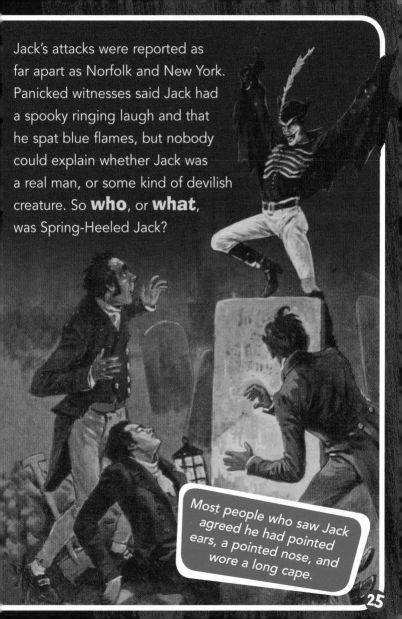

Jack's attacks were reported as far apart as Norfolk and New York. Panicked witnesses said Jack had a spooky ringing laugh and that he spat blue flames, but nobody could explain whether Jack was a real man, or some kind of devilish creature. So **who**, or **what**, was Spring-Heeled Jack?

Most people who saw Jack agreed he had pointed ears, a pointed nose, and wore a long cape.

"The most frightening thing about him was his eyes. They shone like balls of fire."

Jane Alsop,
victim of Spring-Heeled Jack,
February 1838

QUIZ Many of the ✳✳✳✳✳✳✳✳✳ caused by Jack turn

So, have you 'jumped' to any conclusions about Jack yet? Not everybody believes this tall tale, so take a look at their theories ...

◎ Jack's footprints were quite deep, suggesting a human attacker using springs in his shoes.

◎ Many of the injuries caused by Jack turned out to be accidents or animal bites. Did his 'victims' make it up for attention?

◎ *Spring-Heel'd Jack – The Terror of London* was a popular tale in 'penny dreadfuls' – Victorian comic books. These stories may have made people more likely to believe the monster myth.

A Stony Silence

One of the oldest unexplained mysteries in the world is hidden inside an ancient circle of stones called Stonehenge. Although Stonehenge is in Wiltshire, scientists have found that the giant rocks are actually from Wales! So why on earth would anyone move nearly 100 stones (weighing 5 tonnes each!) over 245 miles just to put them in a field?

UN-X-PLAINED FILE

Classification: Stone circle

Location: Wiltshire, England

Date: Building started around 3500 BC

Creators: Ancient Britons

Mystery ranking: A rocky riddle!

FLOATiNG FaCT

Thought stones didn't float? You're wrong! Most of the large stones in Stonehenge were brought from Wales by sea and river, sitting on big rafts!

A bit to your left

Is Stonehenge a UFO landing site?

One theory of why and how Stonehenge got there is that Merlin moved the stones for King Arthur, using magic. Another idea is that the stone arches are mystical gateways to the centre of the earth. Other people think that aliens moved the stones there, to make a kind of giant road sign for UFOs!

29

Scientists now know that Ancient Britons built the stone circle 5500 years ago, but they left nothing to tell us what the circle was for. In about 1650, a man called John Aubrey said he thought Stonehenge was built by an ancient Celtic group of people called Druids, as a place to hold their ceremonies. However, Druids didn't even exist until 1000 years after Stonehenge was built! It is true, though, that the Druids still hold many of their most important ceremonies at Stonehenge. The real reason Stonehenge was built remains as mysterious as the stones themselves.

Druids at Stonehenge

QUIZ One of the oldest ✳✳✳✳✳✳✳✳✳✳ mysteri

The theories about Stonehenge have one thing in common — no one agrees on them! Which do you think is most rock-solid?

◎ Stonehenge was a huge calendar, where time was marked by the movement of the stones' shadows.

◎ Stonehenge was an ancient computer, used for working out when eclipses of the sun and moon would happen.

◎ The goriest theory is that Stonehenge was a temple for sacrifices, and that children or animals were ritually slaughtered there for religious ceremonies. Gruesome!

the world is hidden inside Stonehenge.

Are you even more confused than you were at the start? Let's hope the answer to the quiz doesn't remain an unexplained mystery too! Juggle the first letters of all six answers to make a mysterious word mentioned in this book.

Responsible

Spoons

Dave

Injuries

Dents

Unexplained

Juggle with the letters DDRSIU and you get DRUIDS – mystery solved!

32